Oh!

A Collection of Poems & Short Stories

By George Austin Wills

Rear cover artwork by the author himself ("Bristol Waterfront").

Book compiled by Tony Wills (son of the author).

Illustrations by Rebecca Wills (granddaughter of the author), and a few by the author himself.

Oh!

ISBN: 978-1-80068-140-8

A Cataloguing in Publication record for this title is available in the British Library.

About the Author

George was born in Braunton, Devon, in August 1941 but has spent much of his life in and around the maritime city of Bristol. Now retired, George has enjoyed a checkered career: from tea-making on building sites, filing the jelly in porkpies, to project management for an aerospace company, and transporting nuclear warheads around the UK, to name a few.

However, George never lost his passion for the creative arts – this collection being a testament to this passion.

When George is not painting, writing or sculpting, he can be found contemplating the complexities of life whilst taking the bins out; something very apparent to devotees of his work, as can be seen in the collection.

Oh!

FORWARD

To George Austin, Dad, Boy, Gramps, Dobe, Patch, Epoxy-Resin Wills

Happy 80th Birthday

All our love - to a very talented, unique & much-loved man.

Mary (his beloved and long-suffering wife for over 50 years), Tony & Mark (his sons), Tracy (Tony's wife), Sian, Becky & Sam (Tony's & Tracy's children).

xxx

PREFACE

This book contains a collection of poems and short stories from the prolific Bristol-based poet, writer and artist, George Austin Wills.

It has been compiled with submissions from friends and family who have had the pleasure of receiving his musings over the years, each of whom were delighted to be able to contribute to this unique collection.

So, join me now in reading this work as we go on a journey through often strange, sometimes moving prose; from the fantastical, to the prosaic, but always written with love.

INDEX

Short Poems

Longer Poems

Short Tales

Short Poems

Cyder

I know it's somewhat decadent

To sit here, cyder-drinking

But I've found the wicked apple

Really sharpens up my thinking!

Little Castle

Off for a two-day party

At Clevedon, on the coast

It's in a little castle

I hope it has a ghost!

The Beast

It's taken all my money

The beast within the phone

Left me with less than little

Can't talk, so feel alone

Ode To Fig Rolls

You stole my waistline

Teasing child of grain and fig

Go now, tempt no more

Oh!

Universe

From an inch away

A twig is a universe

For lichen and moss

Goodnight

Well I suppose it's worth a try

But most of my words have
gone to bed

Have shut their bedroom door

And a little note says, "Don't
Disturb!"

I think I'll say no more.

Words

A few words together, and dancing in rhyme?

A modest target, I've plenty of time.

The caffeine's not working

The words will not come!

They've withdrawn their labour

And I'm left here – dumb!

Today

Today I put a palm-tree in a pot

That sounds like something or nothing

But to me it's a lot!

Tradition

I'd better write a poem

'Cos tradition says I must

But all my magic words

Have crumbled into dust!

Morning

'Tis morning, so they tell me

Though I am filled with doubt

'Cos mornings should be beautiful

But my head is full of nowt!

Oh!

Ironing Again

Ironing is Fun!

Ironing is Bliss!

I really cannot take

Much more pleasure than this!

Migraines

One thing to be said for migraine

Is that it paints the night with stars

When I'm putting out the binses

To get rid of the boxes and jars!

Nap

There's a lot to be said for a nap

It will work wonders for a chap

Who's been up since half five

Ten long hours in which I've

Journeyed far, roads and hills

Purchased pasties and some pills.

??? a line lost here- work on it, Wills.

So now, as I've said, for that nap.

Line Up Words

Line up words, and do my bidding

Give me your strengths and skills

Elsewise I'll have your guts for garters

Or I'm not George A Wills!

Grayson Perry

I'm off to look at Art today

By a chap called Grayson Perry

Some say he's a little odd.

A little? Very!

My Phone & I

Me and the phone

We need to recharge

Our dials are both in the Red

The phone will sit in a cupboard

Plugged in

While I take off to my bed

Platypus

There's a small furry thing with a rather large beak

Said "they once spoke of me as a man-made freak!

A fake little jigsaw from various beings

From a bird and a beaver - have I not feelings!

I am a creature, a being complete!

From impossible egg to my big webbed-feet"!

Day Gone

A day gone

A day done

Night has claimed it

Taken the light from it

Draining its warmth

As a vampire, draining its life

5:50 a.m

I didn't mean to be here, I meant to be in bed

But the Sun reached in and teased me

So I came down instead

There's Caffeine now inside me, moving through each vein

Exciting things will happen - if it ever finds my brain!

Oh!

Amazon

We three parcels from Amazon are

Covered in labels we've travelled so
far

Cardboard, blue plastic and
crumpled brown wrap

Conspiring to drag him out of his
nap

BRI

Well that was anti-climactic

My day in the BRI

Except for the coffee and biscuits

Of which I took LOTS, on the sly!

Bins

Looking at all the
binses

And all the soggy
boxes

Squashing it all down

To keep out all the
foxes

The lorry comes at 7
a.m.

I can hear it in the
distance

There's an awful lot
for me to move

I could do with some assistance!

Little Poem

Time for a little poem

So I'm looking for a word

This is ME that's talking

So should it be absurd?

Maybe that's what's expected

Because it's what you've heard

I can do quiet and sober

But 'silly' seems preferred!

Daises

I've declared war upon the daisies

My mowers set to Deconstruct!

There are just a few survivors

The clever ones that ducked!

I've been marching up and
down

Their heads they have been
flying

I'm pretending that I'm deaf

So I cannot hear

Worst Night?

Was that the worst night ever?

Is the question in my mind

As I sit here in confusion

Whilst my brain I cannot find

That questioning is coming

From beneath the kitchen table

I think that's where my brain is

I'd look – if I were but able

My Ironing Pile

Oh, Ironing! Such Joy Domestic!

My pile of clothes is quite Majestic!

It towers over Nailsea Town

Climbers compete to reach its' crown.

Sherpas gather in its shade

Some won't climb it – too afraid!

The treacherous, crumbling, Northern Face

Needs cunning, guile, and feline grace.

Snow and Ice mark the Eastern route

Some say 'tis easy, but the point is moot.

I daren't approach for now it's thawing

Trapped in the ice were creatures – Clawing!

My Pen

There's a lot of lovely words

That live inside my pen

And I manage to coax them out

But only now and then

Sometimes they do my bidding

At odd moments in the night

But mostly trite and silly

Are the ones that see the light.

A Poet?

What, me, a poet? How absurd!

When there's not a single word

Will volunteer to do my bidding

They all remain devoutly hidden.

When I call them to give me verse,

They all conspire to send their worse,

The small, the shallow, the worst-bred

The deformed, the underfed.

When I task them, "Give me Rhyme!"

It seems they think 'twould be a crime.

They deny me, leave me wanting.

That's why I find poems daunting.

Gardening

It's hard to write an ode

(Or some might say a 'ditty')

When you've been a'gard'nin'

And your fingers are all gritty.

There's bits of soil upon this page

All sticking to the ink

And some little creatures crawling

One is red and two seem pink

But I've laid some lovely flat stones

Where there were weeds before

And the blessing coming from this?

I needn't mow there anymore!

In The Light

There's a chill on the hill

It's dark in the Park

But I don't care

Because I'm not there

Not affected by that

I'm here in the light

And the warm

With the cat

Silver Fish

It's not enough,

searching for words,

holding a pen,

waiting to pin them to a page should they pass,

hoping to spear them as you might a fish

that surfaced for an instant to feed.

They swirl,

offering colours and shapes,

movements and moods,

cavorting and teasing,

silver fish beneath the surface of my
mind,

evading my pen. And today?

I spear nothing and they run free.

No Paper No Pen

Ain't got no paper

Ain't got a pen

But to write some words

I have a yen

I'll do them in e-

That doesn't need ink!

And I can e-write

Whatever I think!

But I've been up since four

(well, sort of I s'pose)

And the bits that do 'thinking'

Are back in repose

Errands

There are bins to be put out

There are errands to be run

I've got to buy some porridge

And perhaps a currant bun

There's urgent need of cat-food

(At least that's what they say)

They're keen that I should go now

But THEY'RE not the ones who'll pay!

Back From Errands

I'm back from the errands!

I've stayed mostly dry!

But the cats will not thank me

I WISH they would try!

Art

I shall arise and make some Art!

Or is that just a single part

Of the general confusion

(Verging upon self-delusion)

That permeates my brain and being

Sending common senses fleeing?

Yet again, Self-Inquisition

Strikes, to kill the inspiration

That raised me from my sleeping state

Action! Or 'twill be too late!

Quick! Snatch a pencil, pen, or brush

Generate a hectic rush

Oh!

That takes of me at least my heart

Into the sensual world of Art!

Oh!

'Tis not far from Tuesday morning, Oh!

As I scratch my head for wordses, Oh!

I'm finding nary a one!

I hunt for silly jokses, Oh!

For ways to make them giggle, Oh!

But find – not even a pun!

I'm sat here with my paintbrush, Oh!

And tens of tens of tubeses, Oh!

A'waiting my command!

"Use us to make some artie, Oh!"

"Use us to make your markie, Oh!"

But I'm deaf so I'll do the ironing and put some washing on

More Oh!

*(NPCICTOA(S) day – No Poetry Cos I Can't Think Of
Any (Sorry) day)*

Just a few lines to mark NPCICTOA(S) day, Oh!

A day too important to let it get away, Oh!

(At least that's what I just heard someone say!)

But come to think of it perhaps that was just me, Oh!

(Perhaps I should mix with a more-informed group of people, Oh!)

Whatever, I will respect the Day and commit no Poetry.

I sit here with expectation, Oh!

Awaiting words of Wisdom, Oh!

A'dancing cross the screen.

But all I get is pauses, Oh!

And lots of cross deletions, Oh!

And mutterings obscene.

I wonder what's expected, Oh!

Oh!

As I thread words to a necklace, Oh!

To catch the setting Sun.

Here is a noun of substance, Oh!

Here an adjective full of colour, Oh!

A verb – and my work here is done!

O!

(I have been reading about Japanese Minimal Poetry – its
influence on the following may be apparent)

., Oh!

., Oh!

.!

., Oh!

., Oh!

.!

Milk For My Tea

There's a lot to be said

For staying in bed

But with things to make

'Twould be a mistake

And as for paint

Bed ain't

The place to be!

Oh!

So, I'm up and about

And about to go out

For the milk for my tea

And then my coffee

Which I find

Liberates my mind

And helps me create...

But it's getting late!

So, now I will go...

Oh!!

St. Luke

I've done the binses

Got rid of the tinses

Gone are all boxes

(No sign of the foxes!)

Disposed of the papers

And spoke to the neighbours

Agreed on inflation

And the state of the nation

Came back for a coffee

And then for some tea

Now if, by a fluke,

I can find that St Luke

Oh!

And beg back my gear

I can then persevere

With my urging to paint

(In a manner that's quaint)

And seek good reviews

From some friendly Muse

Words From A Shop

I bought some words,

Jumbled remnants, from the shop

Insultingly under-priced

Unwanted, donated, maybe an act of charity

Or just because it was nearer than the tip

Or some convenient lay-by

A mixture, some used, some overused

Their finish scratched, rubbed through

Some abused, in the ignorance of their abuser

Some virginal, still wrapped, unopened

Not called upon, their usage foreign to their owner

Too many syllables, perhaps, who knows

One, Three & Six

I am trying to pull some words into line

Although I'm so terribly tired

'Cos I was up at one, and three, and six

And it's hard to feel inspired

The line ends in a verb, with a noun in front

That seemed like a workable plan

But the preceding pronouns, and a comma or two

Won't let me be their front-man

They shout of their rights, and refuse to be pushed

'Tween you and me, they're just little hijackers

They're getting their coats, off to new worlds

They'll be writing mottoes - for crackers!

Washing Poem

The Sun is up

So I must wash

All my shirts

And assorted socks

This drying weather

Must not go to waste

Gather up my pants!

I must make haste!

Chuck in some towels

And a hanky or two

Three silly Tees

I'm sure that will do!

Start up the machine

Oh!

Sit down with my tea

In a day I'll be ironing!

That's Heaven for me!

Dealing With The Bins

The bins called me, dragged me cursing from my bed

They leaked icy rainwater onto my feet

I swore as the green-waste lid snapped onto my smallest finger

I trundled all four eighty paces to the road and turned for home

And saw, against a violet sky, the crescent Moon

Sharp enough to draw blood

And Venus, the Morning Star, crackling white, piercing my eyes

And my soul lifted

I owe much to the Bins

Snails In The Margin

I've developed an affection

For old painting styled 'Monastic',

For snails with sword and armour

In a style far from 'Scholastic'

There's rabbits playing bagpipes,

A gold-winged violinist pig

Goat-bodied Kings and Ladies

With mermaids dance a jig

Oh!

I worry for the artists

Whence came those things they drew?

I think they had been sniffing

Something that's in their glue!

Time Beach

Life is a land, built up of Time. Dark seas

With cutting waves fret at its borders,

Breaking our years, heartbeats, minutes, into sand,

Stealing our hours, giving no seconds back

The Time we knew was built from many fragments

Cut by those seas from lives that came before

Taken from them, and turned to stone for our days

To live and love, but sand again before we knew

New land's laid down from what those seas remove,

Building new days, new minutes and new years,

Wide Time-beaches built from our fragments

Places where future lovers shape their lives.

Yet I feel a later You will walk those beaches,

Oh!

Stride Woman-Friday, first-foot, bare-foot, on those sands.

I'll not be there, no longer sharing Time with you,

But I will speak with you still, in the voice of the gulls.

Longer Poems

Methuselah Worm

Do you remember, Methuselah Worm?

Do you remember back then?

Back when ...

... when Rain was a pleasure that brought us to light

Without acid to burn our senses?

Do you remember, Methuselah Worm?

Do you remember back then?

Back when ...

... when the Soil was soft and smooth to the touch

As we made our easy Roads,

and Rain was a pleasure that brought us to light, without acid to
burn our senses?

Do you remember, Methuselah Worm?

Do you remember back then?

Back when ...

... when the Earth was not hot and hard and dry,

And plants grew to give us shade,

and the Soil was soft and smooth to the touch as we made our easy Roads, and Rain was a pleasure that brought us to light, without acid to burn our senses?

Do you remember, Methuselah Worm?

Do you remember back then?

Back when ...

... when our bodies were full and moist and soft

And our only danger the birds,

and the Earth was not hot and hard and dry, and plants grew to give us shade, and the Soil was soft and smooth to the touch as we made our easy Roads, and Rain was a pleasure that brought us to light, without acid to burn our senses?

No Rhythm No Rhyme

I'm looking for a poem

That'll help me say goodnight

But the words they will not line up

Won't fit together right

Though here's a little sense of rhythm

And there's a little bit of rhyme

So I think I'd better use them

And finish – right on time!

I had a little thought

I thought like what I ought

Is to make verse finely wrought

But the trap in which I'm caught

'tis a task with danger fraught

And the risk? I'll end with nought

And then I'd be distraught

Indeed, be overwrought

And the battle which I'd fought

Would lose that which I sought.

Ain't got no rhythm

Ain't got no rhyme

Will have to do poem

Some other time

How can a ditty come to an end

Having said nothing witty

Nor tried to offend?

'Tis a matter of timing

The Hand of the Fates

The timer's gone "Ping!"

My porridge awaits!

'Poemtry'

The world can have sharp edges

It's not always smooth and calm

But under my stone with my eyes shut

The darkness acts as a balm

There's company here unexpected

Words that I thought I'd mislaid

They hid here when they were needed

Safe from abuse in this shade

I'd not meant to hurt or demean them

I'd not known that they could feel pain

But we've talked, and reached understanding

Seems they'll dance for me again

I've agreed that I'll respect them

Oh!

I'll no longer injure their pride

If there's no more 'binses and tinses!'

Then they'll come along for the ride

They're older than me by countless years

And have shaped our laws and our codes

What right have I to torment them

To fit them to trivial odes?

Tomorrow we'll cast aside this stone

And march out together as one

And working together we'll write real prose

And 'poemtry' that will be fun!

Runt Of The Litter

I've been asked to write a story

About some little creature

The weakling of its litter

With no redeeming feature

I'm asked that it find love

I've no imposed constraint

I'm musing now for an approach

What picture should I paint?

A body I shall give him

But a body as of air

His love the first music note

That his kind ever hear

His home an orphan planet

Of which you'll never learn

Lonely, round a nothing star

A thing of no concern

A passing satellite, curious

Out from Earth a thousand years

Sounds out a single sampling pulse

None but our creature hears

Waves pass through his body

which amplifies that sound

His the first voice ere to sing

And for that he's crowned

That one true note that sang

And was never heard again

Gave him stature in his kind

Oh!

No other could attain

That note in him gave ecstasy

That lived in him for life

That one short sweet moment

Stayed with him – lover – wife

A 'Pome'

Brushes to the left of me

Brushes to the right

In front of me the window

And a dark and stormy night

There's music quite hypnotic

And a LOT of Tawney Port

There's a little silver table lamp

Shining on what ought

To be a mini-masterpiece

Of poppies bright and red

But there's only angry crossings-out

I think I'll go to bed

Back in the same position

Oh!

As I was in last night

Gave up on the poppies

Am now using yellow, bright

A dandelion is my goal

Growing up through paving

I gave the poppies my regrets

Spoken loud! I must be raving!

Shopping

I want to have some brekkie

So I need to take a stroll

To buy some bits of bacon

To fill my buttered roll

Other things also are needed

Milk and eggs must not be missed

I don't want to forget them

So I'd better make a list

I'll put down bread and tea-bags

And I'll need some honey, too

Maybe some packs of cat-food

And some tissue for the loo

But I've just looked out the window

Oh!

As I pondered - '?A baguette?'

It's dark - and cold - and windy!

The walk is long and wet

Surely, I'm not as hungry

As I thought I was before

And as I watch the weather

My doubts they grow some more

I think I'll go for – Healthy!

Who needs all that clutter?

I'll settle for the fresh bread roll

(It's a shame there is no butter)

I must go to the shop once more

The shop at the end of the lane

The bird-song makes it a pleasure

But the mud is a bit of a pain.

Bins

'As I trundle out the wheelie

I ponder "Is this really

Enough reason for existence,

Have we not made ANY distance

From when we all dressed in fur

That we'd stolen from a bear

With weapons made of sharpened bone

And some others made of stone

This whilst knowing all the time

That on US the bear might dine!"

But then an inner voice says "Wills

You've just GOT to take your pills!

Step back onto solid ground

Oh!

Let's not hear another sound!

No more of these silly rambles

Your mind 'tis in a shambles!

So, do your duty by the bins

Out with the card and with the tins

Then come back, do something clever

Set out on some bold endeavour

Settle at your desk again

Arm yourself with brush or pen

Mark some paper, have some fun

Exciting colour or some clever pun

Shape yourself, get back your pride

And if you fail?

At least you tried!'"

No Ration Book

She took it, my sister did, bitch sister, sister witch

Took my ration book, hid it before I returned to
school,

Dreading it, and now for a month I am
defenceless

The tuck-shop open-sesames at five and we
dive, en-mass, for the doors

But not for me, this time, this month, the rock
or the mints, bulls-eyes or aniseed balls,

No near-chocolate Five-Boys, no Spangles, no
other bright-dyed baubles

No dentists' friend, no tooth-decaying, jaw-
stretching, placebo,

No exchange for my talisman half-crown – "'No
ration book? Sorry. Next!"

No shield for me bought from those bright,
tempting, sweet-scented, boxes,

Oh!

No wheel-sized Wagon Wheel to ransom my
property back from Shaw,

(So testosteroned he shaved from eleven, and
keeps a cut-throat)

No sugar-laden currency to buy protection,
shelter against the older boy,

A singularity, yards wide, said to bully his
parents as well, for the practice

With tuck-shop bribes, I wouldn't be hit, my
bedding would not disappear,

No stud-raking 'accident' at rugby, no "Wills
said..." to credulous, cane-wielding, masters

But now,

Without it ... Sister witch, bitch, If I survive, I
think I'll set your hair alight ...

...again

Mediterranean Bay

Through time, men have killed here for these beaches

Greeks, Arabs, Romans, Turks and Byzantines.

Fighting for gold, or for what somebody preaches

Dying beneath these cliffs and twisted pines

Pirates left here, sailing round that headland

To loot fat traders and bring back their spoil

Risking their lives against ships heavy manned

For foreign slaves and wine and olive oil

After the Eastern Empire, Venice reigned

And built this back-drop fort above the bay

But, looting, stole a Sultans harem and

The island was the price they had to pay

But in the quiet years, among this wasting,

Oh!

Lovers sat here beneath these twisting pines

Eating, like us, this cheese and bread, tasting

Like us, these sweet and scented island wines

Potters Wheel

You thought me clay,

Inert, Amorphous, Safe

Churched, you took me as the potter takes the clay

To shape me on your wheel, then fire me

Fix me in new form, defined as yours

While still clay I could be anything

For any potter

I could adapt, could not be broken, could not harm

But thrown, then tempered by your fire

I can now, without breaking, be one thing only

That which *you* would have me be

But I have learned to break, to make an edge

That cuts and wounds you

Oh!

What am I now, you ask

As you bleed.

I only know what I *would* be

I would be clay again

To shape on my own wheel

Queue

I'm in a queue

To join a queue

I'm number thirteen thousand

Eight hundred eighty-two

In the queue

To join a queue

A little break in Spain

A few hours on a plane

Friendly bars and sandy beaches

Far from greyness, far from rain

Instead? In Panic Mode

Typing in my access code

To battle with insurers distant

Oh!

Their system clogging under load

And I'm still in Panic Mode

Typing useless access code

I'm not having any fun

They continue me to shun

But progress, slow, IS being made

I'm now at One Three Eight Eight ONE!

But still not having any fun

With their system set to "SHUN!"

The Dragon

There's a Dragon in the cupboard at the bottom of the stairs

And I'm the only one who knows

He's red glowing eyes, a sharp pointy tail

And flames coming out of his nose

and then -

Now *it's **Me*** in the cupboard at the bottom of the stairs

With the brushes and the Dyson cleaner

The dragon is sleeping in my bed now

'Cos he's got a whole lot meaner!

and then -

Did I mention the dragon? Not many know

I'd one that I kept – as a pet

I had to release him, he got hiccups one day

Burned Backwell, then roasted the vet!

Oh!

and then -

Talking of creatures, red ones *or* green

Did I tell you what this morning was seen?

From the ashes of Backwell (still glowing bright)

Came varied reports of a wonderful sight

All say that, seen clearly in the blue smoky air

A phoenix was rising, its flight so rare

That hope was engendered, and smiles were born

But from those who weren't there

There was nothing but scorn

Day of Oh!

I'm told 'tis Saturday mornin', Oh!

But I feel like Thursday fortnight, Oh!

And I shouldn't have left me bed!

There's bears and little things green and furry, Oh!

And hyphens and colons and things sort of verbal, Oh!

A'spinnin' around in me 'ed!

Ow!

Twas on a Friday morning, Oh!

I did behold my note-book, Oh!

And took my pen in hand

But words refused my summons, Oh!

They hid in dark recesses, Oh!

Too deep within my mind

They've not All gone a'hiding, Oh!

There's still a few remaining, Oh!

They're trapped within my pen!

They've left me 'but' and 'and' and 'Oh!'

Still doing what I tell them, Oh!

But what's the use of that!

'Tis on a Sunday morning, Oh!

Ought I would do some painting, Oh!

So I took off to my room,

But the cat was in my chairie, Oh!

And wouldn't budge an inchie, Oh!

So I went off for me tea

'Tis on a Monday morning, Oh!

I'm putting out the binses, Oh!

And having so much fun!

So I jump on cardboard boxes, Oh!

And squash the little tinses, Oh!

(Though I'm careful with the glass!)

Then I stack a crate on the wheelie, Oh!

And top it with another, Oh!

And pull it eighty paces, in the rain!

And now 'tis Tuesday morning, Oh!

Still messing with the stringses, Oh!

And holes in bits of wood!

"They think he's lost his marbles!", Oh!

"Don't know what he's a'doin'!", Oh!

And who's to disagree?

'Tis on a Wednesday morning, Oh!

I don't know what I'm doing, Oh!

But what's the News in that?

I want to do some painting, Oh!

But I want to do some writing, Oh!

The answer? - put paint in my pen!!

Tis now a Sunday morning, Oh!

So I survey my options, Oh!

Do I try to save my soul?

To bare all in confession, Oh?

To bend my knee in Chapel, Oh?

Or my elbow in the pub?

The bells are Sunday-ringing, Oh!

So I survey my options, Oh!

How to save my soul from Hell?

To bare all in confession, Oh?

To bend my knee in Chapel, Oh?

Or my elbow in the Bell?

I got the word from Google, Oh!

They say this stuff is doggerel, Oh!

And has little right to be!

I'll seek some other verdict, Oh!

I think I'll ask my readers, Oh!

And see if they agree.

I've mowed down all the daisies, Oh!

And trimmed off all the grass

And now I take my wages, Oh!

Its cyder, in a glass!

Notes To An Impatient Reader

I have struggled all day with words

To compose, and give you, a rhyme

But they've been marshalled against me

And it's been a waste of my time

It was to have started "Good Morning!"

And talked, perhaps, of my Night

But a.m. merged into p.m.

And still they didn't look right!

So, I prodded some more at the nouns

Pronouns, conjunctions, and rhythm

To try to bring them to order

But there's nothing I could do with'em

So now I must say that I've failed

Oh!

And apologise for the delay

As darkness creeps over my shoulder

I'll put my laptop away

So, the words that set out to greet you

And welcome you into the day

Arrive under cover of darkness

Poetry isn't Childs Play!

Not Silly

I'll set out to write a poem

That has no trace of 'silly'

If I slip in some madness

They will make protest, shrilly!

I'll use words long and heavy

There'll be no trace of "Oh!"

There'll be Greek and Roman phrases

And with virtue it will glow!

But in this I sense a problem

Would it be seen as true to type?

Would they think that it *was* my work?

Would some *other* get the hype?

I might not get my due acclaim

The respect due for my striving

I would soon fall from favour

My reputation swiftly diving

No! This is not my future!

I will not let it be!

I'll hurry back to "Silly!"

And then they'll know it's Me!

Oh!

Waking In The Morning

I believe in Evolution, I go through it every day

From before the Dawn's first glimmer – it's a price I have to pay

Every night does drain from me all Man's progress biologic

Evolve again is what I must - from the Proterozoic!

I close my eyes each night as something of human stock

But somewhere in the darkness, forces dark reset my clock

Return me to times primeval, in that deep organic soup

From which I must find my way, in a never-ending loop

The force that does debase me leaves me as a single cell

Then I'm alone in darkness, as the bottom of a well

But I find a safer place, under a friendly little rock

And, in the mud, there's silence - save the ticking of that clock

Another force I can't resist now prods me in my dreaming

Oh!

Lifts up my rock and wakes me, bids me to do its' scheming

It's a process in whose details I feel I'm too well versed

Thirty thousand times before this path has been rehearsed

Progress each day does vary, sometimes I do reach Sapient!

If not, then some lesser place on that upward gradient.

But now I'm forced my role to play, I hear my curtain call

Please let this day be one where I pass Neanderthal!

So, following Darwin's Pathway, through stumbling turn and halt

I single-cell my way, through seas of sour salt

Seeking company in darkness, I link with common kind

And now I'm multi-cellular, with a body that is spined!!

I browse on smaller creatures, suck them in without a pause

But there are creatures after ME, and they have all got claws!

The day grows older, and demands that I evolve some more

To face the tasks awaiting me on mornings distant shore

A little further progress now, and I'm the one who's armed

Those that used to prey on me begin to be alarmed

But I seek more, grow legs and crawl, they'll call me Trilobite

There's an awful lot of us down here, I'm quite the socialite!

Ambition calls, tells me "There's more, search for a new horizon!

You must make haste, use all those legs, the Sun will soon be rising!"

I take in caffeine by osmosis, prepared by some robot hand

It brings increases awareness and my first crawl on dry land

I'm early here and find that it's much too hot and dry

But things improve, I prosper, as millennia fly by

I might have been a vegan, but before plants were provided

I'd acquired a taste for squealing things, my future was decided

But with first taste of mammal (small) my diet was decided

Oh!

I see I'm on the wrong branch of Darwin's famous tree

Find I have arms, prehensile tail – this is the one for me!

I swing across, another branch, different competition

And from somewhere deep inside me, a nudging of ambition

Life in the trees is good for me – I spend time as a sloth

But the light of Dawn's demanding that I make further growth

Life downside-up, and easy prey, does not appeal to me

Though it's with trepidation that I climb down from my tree

The trees fade, I'm in grassland and now I am walking proud

Well, I'll admit my brow is low and my back is somewhat bowed

Though, compared with Trilobites, I'm simply oozing noblesse

I'm still far from Homo Sap and must make further progress

But now I'm seen as prey again, and I've a sense of fear

So, a long stick, fire-hardened, goes before me as a spear

Then I'm moving faster, I make pictures in dark caverns

Oh!

Lots of posing animals, and hands and feet as patterns

A moment as Neanderthal, but that I quickly leave

I've made it! Homo Sapiens! There's no more to achieve!

But this has taken far too long, the thought does give me pain

'Tis time for bed which means, alas – I do it all again!

Sweet Charity

'K'ching!'

A bright cheerful brass bell, and in from the street

Door closes behind us, now safe from the sleet

Three staff smile from the counter, and one from the store

Business is quiet, they were hoping for more

Bridget and Kathy, Rebecca and Claire

They watch as we wander, the only ones there

Shelves full of china, shelves full of brass

Shelves with ceramic and metal and glass

Lined up around us pristine or time-worn

Cast out of our lives, unloved and forlorn

Things smelling of wardrobes, of years in the dark

Clothing in styles pre-dating the Ark

Oh!

We see items of paper, of canvas, of wood

Things knitted and hammered and painted and glued

A stopperless carafe, with five glasses from six

A Barbie, a Ken, and some little toy bricks

Cutlery, virgin since the day it was gifted

A squashed piece of silver whence sugars once sifted

A small seaside piece labelled, wrongly, as Delft

A book with MY name in SHE brought from MY shelf!

Books by an author whose name I recall

But stacked out of reach by someone too tall

Photograph albums with family ghosts

Pictures of aunties, and far foreign coasts

'The Devil Hates Kansas', it says on this book

Oh, God, a mirror, that's ? not ? how ? I ? look?

Some left-over soaps, and bath-salts from Gran

Oh!

Maracas, and egg cups, a teapot and fan

Some Dynasty blouses and fifty-waist jeans

A small silver hip-flask from someone with means

Shells stripy and spiky, bought on the Med

Some wooden creation brought straight from a shed

A bright red handbag and a small fabric purse

Attacked not by moth but by something much worse

A lightning conductor and glass fishing-floats

Bright pink slippers and zipperless coats

Souvenirs come here, once bought to impress

But failed in that purpose, so here now they rest

From Egypt, Sorrento, from Rome and Oman

From Majorca, Minorca, from Crete and Milan

From Italy, Spain and, much further away

From Mexico, Cuba, and the U. S. of A.

Oh!

That's enough for me now, though the weather's still poor

Just one more shelf, on the way to the door

What's that purple thing? – yes, a nice little pot

What's it say? Poole, England? Surely not!

Let's to the till, give Kathy the pound

Forty on e-Bay, or more, I'll be bound!

'K'ching!'

Oh!

Short Tales

Girl in the Princess Outfit

He looked. I saw him look. She caught his eye, so bright in the rain; he looked at her for a second, then at me for another. A puzzled look, back at her, then away, kept walking away from us, from me. Just like that night, interest then indifference. Eleven years. He made me feel special; he had money then, the clothes, the car, oh that car. My man had none of those and for a week or two the glamour won me. Long enough.

My husband spoke to her this morning as we left. 'My Princess', he called her, 'My Princess'. Princess, yes, but not his.

He loves another man's child and doesn't know it. Her father just passed us, a moment's attention, and then gone. A torment in me, for I should hate him for false promises and abandonment.

I have hated him for years but now, at that moment, I felt thankful, for though he is not king nor prince nor duke he gave me my beautiful Princess who would be nowhere but for him, maybe still waiting in limbo to be another woman's child, not mine.

I thank him.

Derelict Building

Ghosts walk. Floor gone, bedrooms merge with living space, ghosts of wallpaper and of paint, ghosts of toys and of people. Memories are ghosts, as insubstantial and as impossible to capture or to retrieve. Damp. Sunlight intruding where it was never meant to reach, not from that angle. Damp where ghosts remember dry. Cold where ghosts remember warmth.

They still walk then, while in the now, sun strikes through the roof and through the walls that kept them private, kept their secrets, the facades that helped maintain their pretences and their posturing in public while they could live a very different private secret life. Paper peels from the rain, hangs like party streamers but no party now. Childs drawings revealed as floral print droops towards welcoming open cellar.

A child crying, screaming, now, here, would be heard through the spaces where walls and windows muffled before. But the need for help, support, comfort is gone, is itself a ghost. If the walls had been as unsubstantial, the windows just empty squares then, his cries might have been heard, might have brought help and comfort. But the façade, the walls and windows and curtains stood strong and silenced and betrayed him - then. Only his ghost is here to be comforted now.

In At The Deep End

The deep end has the diving board, I go to the end with trepidation, fear, unknowing - like the gang-plank you walk from a pirate ship, for their entertainment, the skull and crossbones on black above you, symbol of death, speaking of decay and dismemberment, speaking of bones in the ground.

Skeletons being disinterred by archaeologists, two being exhumed together, shown together in a museum case, with grave goods, jewellery, beakers, weapons, impression of textile on hardened clay... A neatly-printed screed streams down the back of the case, behind and beside them. "The male, a warrior, his spear of (such and such), his sword of bronze, amber beads beside him...". And the female? "The tradition then was for his wife or a slave to be sacrificed and buried with him to serve him in the afterlife." And so on.

And at night, in the museum, a wandering consciousness, a voice, a plea – "It was not like that! I was the warrior. That is my spear they give him, that is my sword! What was he? I won those scalps! Those rings were mine! He was a dog of a man, a nothing, a less-than-nothing! Why did they bury him with me, why? Me, a slave? Me, a mere wife? The insult to me, to my House! How could my clan have allowed it, surely, they fought against the insult – unless...

An Old Map

A map can tell you a truth, or even the truth – or it can lie to you. You might suspect it early in your journey, as soon as you start and find that the bay you intended for your landing is a rocky headland, when you step into a marsh where good land is shown.

There might be, midway in your intended journey but a finale to your actual one, a second (if you are lucky) of burning agony and a curse for the cartographer who omitted the warning "Here Be Dragons". Or maybe the map seems to stand you in good stead for your whole journey.

The landing is good, the beach as gently shelving as the map said. It guides you round the swamp. The dragon doesn't get you because, informed, you went around the other side of the hill. You find the tavern and shelter where you had been promised them. But, at the last, the map does betray you. Four paces from the three palm trees, where the cross is marked, you dig and find, not the chest, not the chalice, not the gold – but the Dragon's eggs, and She is behind you.

Goodbye.

An Old Map Revisited

Maps equal hope, places to go, to plan for, places to leave, goals to achieve, plans to make, expectations and dashed hopes.

You are shown crosses on a map, drawn there to make the thing more valuable, more transactable, less honest and more treacherous. You buy the map, you subscribe to a false belief, false hope, and make your life around it.

You sail away for a year and a day to the land where the cross says your future wealth lies – and there is nothing. Or worse, there are signs that someone else who bought a copy of the same map before you did has been here already, has dug where you would have dug, has lifted what you would have lifted, and there had been treasure.

The gold you have been calling yours for a year and a month and a day is gone, is being spent in giving comfort and status to an interloper, an intruder, a thief who has now stolen the rest of your life from you.

You were not the only on with a map, not the only one with an eye on the cross, but one step behind them was too late.

An Unforgettable Face

Why would you find one face unforgettable as against the tens of thousands you will hold in your memory for only a year or a month or a second or less?

There must be something imprinting about it, maybe the face itself has unusual characteristics, blemishes, wrinkles, eyes, ears. Or it might be association that fixes it for ever in your mind, you remember it as part of a setting, an ecstasy, a reprimand, an achievement, a drama, and it fixes itself somewhere, a fixed and un-erasable pattern in the confused network of cells and synapses in your brain so engraved that only the grave will smooth it away.

His face I will never forget, though I have spent blank hours in the darkness wishing I could. I hadn't seen him before, at least not this close.

There were no unusual characteristics to etch it on my mind – perhaps the eyes might have done so, but the lids were closed, the whole face totally relaxed, and I will never know their colour, nor want to. It was not ecstasy or intimacy either. It was the association that did it, the drama – and the horror. I will remember it for the fact it was no longer part of his body. Or of his skull. Held out to me, bloody, peeled from him, gifted to me after the chase as it were the brush of the fox blooding me after my first hunt.

Cornish Women

I smell of fish. I always smell of fish and of this oil. I will always smell of fish, like my mother did and her mother, and that is how my daughter will smell.

There was a woman yesterday, was it, or maybe Monday. She smelled of roses and the fur she wore, that had its own scent, its own texture.

She will never smell of fish. When she is dead and in her grave, she will be remembered as smelling of roses. My memory will smell of fish. And the oil. Even on Sunday, in my best, such as it is. They know my trade.

They sit above us in chapel, in the gallery, smelling of roses and lilies and tobacco. We below, beneath them, packed in these pews like boxed fish and smelling of it. It is not enough.

When will my time come to smell of roses? Never. Pouring the oil, crushed from the offal. The fish won't like the smell of roses or the touch of fur and a lover who does not smell of fish or the touch of a man's hands soft not scarred by net or line or hook and calloused by salt water and why do they wrinkle their noses as they pass me in the street?

They need me, me and mine, their money to buy the scent of roses and the touch of fur is earned by what I do, and my man does and what my daughter will do, and they still scorn me in the street and sit away from us in chapel.

By what right do they scorn us? We work, and they see the benefits. They worship the same God and read of the same disciples as us. Peter was a fisherman – he would not have smelled of roses or fur.

He would have smelled of fish.

Longer Tales

The Hunt

Killing the eland had been a mistake. From the ease with which he had been able to stalk and to ambush it, from the readiness with which its spirit flew when his spear passed pierced its lungs, brought the scarlet froth to its mouth, he should have doubted it. But they had not fed for four days other than on roots and carrion, and there were young and two pregnant females.

They had to eat now.

The alpha-female of the group took the hunters knife, ripped the kidneys from the warm carcass and handed them to him in her bloody fist, the providers' trophies by right. The blood ran to his chest as he ate, chewing only enough to reduce the hot mass to chunks he could swallow.

Three days before, the antelope also had eaten unwisely. Parasites lay dormant on a leaf, encysted and waiting. The eland had been unlucky. The leaf had been missed by others, could have been missed now, but it wasn't. Chewing and swallowing were the signals the dried spores needed. A war was fought, won, and lost within the animal. The animal was dying. Unspent ammunition from that war, complex chemical strings in its kidneys, would change the hunter's mind forever.

Oh!

The first night they sent, walking through his head, ghosts of things dead and of things yet to live. He screamed at them, struck at them with his spear. It seemed like smoke against the harsh reality of the visions. Fear had him pushing away from the spectres as if to find safety within the rock walls of their lair, not believing that only he could see them, incredulous that the group was not running and screaming also.

In their fear of him, the clan threw him from the cave, though it took five to do it, and they barred his return with fire and spears. The second attack was more subtle.

Ideas, images, questions and answers, all new to a mind that till now could only afford to live in the present, where survival lay. There was a new awareness in him, a questioning, and a gnawing hunger for something without name. Neither food nor sex he craved, not warmth or security, but something that he now knew was hiding within his mind.

On the third night he found the question, and on the fourth he had the answer, that man had it in him to be as the gods and could command and destroy. Between those two nights something sensed his mind. A guardian, if you will, the Watcher, recognised danger in that questioning, in those thoughts, and moved in his direction, alerting its Master as it came. And in that fourth night, when the answer burned in his mind and he tried to share it with his peers, the dogs, the stars and the night, his tribe rejected him again, for now they truly feared him and what his eyes said.

A sooty eye-straining light, guttering, shaping and distorting shadows on the sensual water-carved curves of the rock-face.

When he had worked here before there had been a light, held by a boy now too much in fear of him. No one would share his darkness now. A palette of colours, greasy black from fat and soot, greens from the forest, red from earth and clay burnt in the fire - these would tell what he knew.

The rock wall held all he had said in the past, for these animals and people and hands and feet and suns and trees that recorded his previous days - these were a language. Not sympathetic magic, not fetishism, they were history, achievements, and now his new truth, to be recorded if only to exorcise the pain from his brain.

Fanaticism in his eyes and a screaming in his head, he marched his symbols along the limestone. They must know! Someone must listen! His mind could not survive the voices otherwise. Ten more symbols to go, eight more, seven more, and then the Watcher arrived.

The hunter did not see him, not because of the darkness or his concentration but because he had no physical substance. Only a Watcher, only biding time till its Master came, but it knew that the man must be stopped, the truth must be protected from the minds alive at this time. To delay the man it could do little, but only a little was needed.

Air thickened around the lamp, formed a barrier, and in a second the flame used what oxygen was left inside, and died. The man cursed and groped in his pouch for flint and stone.

When it was lit a third time the Watcher knew it need do no more, for its Master had arrived. The artist, suspiciously guarding the flame with his hand, looked around, trying to cast light into the recesses of the cave, knowing himself watched. He would see nothing, though, for the Master, though it had the strength to shape worlds, had no more substance than the Watcher.

Still unsettled, the artist turned again to his work, and then screamed to see his latest symbol fading from the rock. Stunned, he saw it disappear completely, saw its predecessor fading, gone. He threw himself at the wall to protect the next, a gazelle with its head and horns turned just the way needed to give his exact meaning, covered it with both hands, to protect his work, his truth.

To his left other symbols faded and cleared. Sobbing, he lifted his hands, and saw only bare rock. On the whole wall, nothing remained of his truth. Yet even this was not enough for the Master. The hunter heard a soft gentle voice, full of regret. "I am so sorry", they spoke into his mind, "so truly sorry". He took the torment from the mind of the artist, gave him peace for a moment, and then took his life. The question must not be asked yet, must not be answered. Man needs his gods and must not yet join them.

The Watcher

The horizon sent her false images again, of water, of greenery and movement. Tempting images, the Devil's work.

She knew there were sand, brittle scrub, and the rock behind her throwing back the sun's burning. There was nothing more, no moisture, no foliage, no-one, her only company the lizard that shared this recess in the south-facing cliff.

She felt momentarily flattered that the Devil spent so much effort tempting her, then felt mortified over such self-awareness. She was here solely for communication with her God. Self was a sin. She would need penance for that, but later. Lotus-posed, she focussed again on the horizon, forcing her eyes to see through the illusions to the beautiful sterility that was the truth.

She had known of the bones and leathery dryness of her predecessors, their lives abandoned in this desert in their own search for understanding, each seeking to be the one to find the path to their God. She had visited each cave or hut or cleft rock that had seen them fail and had brought their mummies to her shelter.

She had arranged their skulls in a semicircle of smiles and silent screams, so she could summon their voices back that they might now work together in her search.

Days had passed now, more than she knew. She had not counted the times the sun seared her skin and her mind, or the times the nights froze her reducing supply of water. She had induced hallucination from which the skulls had spoken to her, their tenants telling of their insights and their failures, the cul-de-sacs of abortive thought in which they had trapped themselves. These were her guides in her search.

None of them had thought to call on their predecessors in this desert; each had started from their personal zero. She was different, they had been her vanguard. Together now, they could succeed where separately they had failed. She had called from each of their ghosts their thoughts and conclusions, their failures and successes. She knew now what avenues had proved sterile and what had hinted at achievement. She knew what mirage and distraction were. She would find the gods.

There are doors in the human mind. Some open at a touch, if you can but find them. To other openings the way is devious, and they are hidden and barred, more likely stumbled into than found by design. Very few minds pass here, and fewer return intact.

Driving her mind back deeper into visions, she became as one with her predecessors, the stronger still, the leader, but part of a whole. That combined mind found one of those barred doors and broke through it. They found more than she had been seeking.

She saw that Man was limiting himself seeking communion with the gods, that instead he was meant to be as them. There was exultation in her mind, the realisation that humility and self-deprivation were not needed, that ego counted after all. She must tell. The Order must know that Man's turn to be worshipped rather than to kneel was within reach.

The Watcher had heard the barred door open. He started towards her.

But she could not move. Starvation and dehydration had robbed her body while her mind ignored its protests. She was fixed in the lotus. There was no food left, nor any water.

Her mind, returning from where she had driven it, was alert now and told the other truth, that she would die here, and soon. But what she had found must not die with her. They must know! How to communicate, how to record it? She had no pen, no parchment, and no disciple to carry the message. Her now-lucid mind, knowing it need care no longer for the fading body, showed her a way.

With a steady hand she took the nearest skull and, without ceremony or apology, smashed it on the rock beneath her.

The Watcher found her dead.

Beside her lay the bone shard she had used to open her veins. Written in the last of her blood, and already baked into the rock wall, was her message, Man's pathway to the gods. Her ego had triumphed - the message bore her name. He was a gentle soul, relieved at not having to take her life, but the words must be destroyed.

He paused for a while, thought, and was gone.

Moments later a gentle breeze moved, fingered her clothing. It picked up strength, moving sand around her, then stronger again, rolling the skulls together and mounding sand over them. Fiercer yet, until quartz grains screamed horizontally against the rock, tearing from it the message that could liberate Man.

As wind faded the lizard came out of shelter and continued its own search for meaning.

The Clown

Thank God I have another face to put on to hide behind hide the lines where will I go after the show where will I come from tomorrow and tomorrow painting on tears over the tears and they changed the locks and I still have stuff there Helen's stuff she'll kill me they'll sell it to get their flesh damn that's wrong I wasn't looking one side's up and one side's down they'll laugh at me for the wrong reasons a laugh is a laugh is a laugh and after I will wipe off the sad and there will be sad underneath one sad face on the tissues in the bin and one to go home with whose home where's home and we were happy there I thought then she just wasn't there any more yes John five minutes I'll be ready sorry wonder if he'll let me sleep here till I get things sorted wonder how many lives start going downhill with those words just till I get things sorted just till what I wonder where Helen is would she let me stay with her that wouldn't work would it and anyway she'd want her stuff and I'm dead if she knows what's happened to it perhaps that would do me a favour telling her then *finito benito* whoever Benito was if anyone God I could do with a laugh that's my job isn't it come on make me laugh its what you're paid for you bastard

Another one, as if he hasn't suffered enough already!

Where to go where to go where to go my whole life is in that bag and what was still there when they changed the locks where's the nose my hand is shaking I can't get the line right my eyes aren't the same I know the children won't care but I will care yes I'll be ready five minutes yes five what do they want out of me would they care if they knew they'll sell my life out of the flat for fifty quid and I wont exist anymore and oh god under the floor if they find that I'm in the shit I told them I could get the money I was lying but they didn't know that they should have believed me I'm an actor for god's sake a bloody actor I've done Hamlet that bastard Carver wrote 'I'd done Hamlet to death' that was cruel bugger that's another bulb gone now I'm painting in shadow and I can't get it right cheap bloody place and poor bloody money the dancers get more than I do I bet they don't get evicted and they could sell themselves if it came to it I couldn't sell myself to pay the rent that's what Helen said before she left and Christ her stuff was still in there she's going to kill me she won't see that again serves her right for going and where did she have to go to just like that she must have planned it staged that row hadn't thought that before where did she sleep that night I'm ready I'm ready I'm coming and after this where am I going?

The Coin Man

We are following a coin. It's been done before by others, is considered trite, hackneyed, but – we are following a coin, our coin. It is held by a woman, held with three others, and is being traded for cosmetics, scent, powder. She hopes that for a brief while these will disguise what age and the sun have taken from her. From the moment she hands over the coins she fades from our story – maybe we hope she was right. We won't know – she has been dead two thousand years.

The guildsman who had blended the scent and ground the powders that she bought added more coins to those she gave him and bought oils and aromatic herbs from a traveller from the north.

Our coin became one of many then and joined them in the thonged and tasselled satchel the traveller kept, slung over his shoulder but under his clothes, bronze our coin nudged, and more copper like itself, and silver, and much gold (he was a prosperous man, and near to settling down on the coast, away from his wife).

Myriad faces peered at it, sneered at it, ignored it, from the other coins. Kind faces, cruel faces, stupid faces, all transient in their power, however absolute and permanent it had once seemed, some dead a hundred years or more, remembered now only in these coins and from statues turning to sand in the desert.

Two days later, between the next town and the one beyond that, the traveller died for the bag.

His ghost laughed at them as they kicked his body in their anger, stripped his clothing, and scattered his trade goods from his baggage. They overturned stones for it, dug randomly into the loose sand with the spears that had killed him, then gave up their search, taking only his horse and ass, leaving him and his merchandise to the sun and the wind. Where is it right now, this coin? In the ground again, with a partner of the same age and coinage, base copper, sealing a dead mans' eyes, unwanted fare for a Ferryman who isn't coming. But that is a long time after the traveller's ambush and his murder, the vultures squabbling, and children collecting his finger-bones for their games.

The prize rested in its hollowed space, under the yellow-flowered shrub the traveller meant for a landmark should he survive the pursuit. While the bag aged and embrittled, the coins stayed as they had been, the gold kept its shine, the silver blackened but slightly, for the sand was dry and the air was purer then. But the robbers aged and died, blackened and embrittled. Their children followed them.

The coins fared better.

Every year, since well before these events, shepherds and drovers from the greener lands in the hills had made an annual trek to the markets in these towns, driving sheep in their thousands along a thousand-year-old slot, thirty generations at least, thirty fathers and thirty sons old. They used the same track as the trader had - it was drover children who found his bones and rags, took his fingers as toys.

Every year minds only on the sheep and on the routine of setting and striking camp, they passed the bag, unnoticed even when it lay on the surface for two whole years and part of another. It had been exposed to the elements, laid bare by the scouring wind, but no eyes saw it. Piqued at men's indifference to the opportunity it had given them, the wind buried it again, deeper this time, and for longer.

One year, when even the shrub had recently died, only its erect corpse to cast a shadow, a herder's son found the bag, hammered a tent peg through it as they pitched camp for the night. He dug to see what had resisted him in what he had expected to be merely soft sand.

On another day he might merely have moved the peg to one side, another location, and who knows when or by whose hand the bag would have been brought to daylight. But he dug, found the corner of the bag, with his fingers before his eyes, for it was dusking rapidly, pulled, and the bag broke, giving him one corner and a gold coin. His eyes widened, and he inhaled to shout for his family, to come and look.

Then he bit and ate the words, and did move the peg, a few inches only, and smoothed the hole with fragment of the bag in it - for he remembered his father and elder brothers back in the warmth of the animals, getting drunk while he worked. He remembered his fifteen years and his ten drives, ten weeks each year of extra beatings, little food, the sheep to be worshipped, sleeping outside the family tent for he was not a favoured son.

He saw that the coins he had felt under the sand without lifting them were the only door out of his current life that he would find, other than death. If he had completed the shout he had started would have seen none of their value, only the drunkenness and the gaudies they would have bought the others. He bit his lip and was ready to tell them his small cry had been from pain from a misguided hammer, but no one cared, no-one asked, and he kept his secret.

That night he laid his bedding by that peg - It was the exposed side of the tent, and those others for whom there was no room inside slept in its lee, which suited him. For three hours he dug, with fingers and his small dull knife, and for each of those hours he pulled over a hundred coins from the shifting, sliding, sand. But for the point of the peg having driven one corner of the bag deeper, away from him, he would have had another seven and twenty, but only three of them were of gold, though he did not know it. Sometimes in later life he had 'what If?' dreams of that time - had there been one more coin or a thousand, were there only coins or were there weapons, jewels? - 'What If?" is the world's best paint-box - but those twenty-seven would have made no difference to him, the more-than- three-hundred carried his entire destiny in them. It was two thousand years before wind and tank-tracks and explosions brought the rest to the surface again, but our coin went with the boy.

Pockets were no use to a boy without possessions and none expected. Their normal attire was as if bandaged in rags, he more so than the others, because of his place in their order. This was of more use to him than pockets, for the tune of three hundred coins jingling in a pocket is strange music around a drover's son on a desert trail. Three hours to get all the coins he could, bring them up only singly, so that no two should rattle, and over an hour more binding them into his rags so that they would not move to betray him.

And he smiled the next day, and the one after, even during a beating just for being in the way, so much so as to earn him another, for who likes beating a son if it seems he is enjoying it? One blow that knocked him down dislodged three coins, but he sensed it, and lay as if stunned while the hand under him gathered them in again.

When the herder's left the market town three days later, they left the sheep, and what moneys the taverns and the willing women had not taken from them, but they also left the boy. They searched for him for a short while, but his plans had been three days in the making, and they were in a hurry to get back to their village. Anyway, with no sheep to drive now, they could do without him. As to needing him on the next years drive, well, they had a god to look to for help, and another to curse if it was not forthcoming - and there were other children who could start to earn their keep.

Shrewd he was, and well-funded now - if he and it lay idle, but that was neither his destiny nor his intention. He had moved well, carefully but well and gained influence. It was in the sixth year his family, which he had seen in each of the droving seasons since, recognised him and tried to reabsorb him and his wealth by force - but he had friends then, and the drovers left without him again.

Six years on again and he owned the town, but no longer wanted it. It was not the large world it had seemed that first night on the loose with his money, now he knew it for just an insignificant corner, an unimportant region of a struggling country, and he felt great destiny in himself. He was only partly right in this - it was not him but his seed that destiny wanted for the board game it plays with us. But till that seed was sown, and the child nurtured, destiny would protect him as its own.

He spent our coin the first night. He spent it twice more unknowingly in the years before he left the town, and each time it meant less to him. The last time he threw it to a beggar, not for charity, for he had learnt none, but to impress a woman, and even then, he had made sure it was the smallest coin he had.

But on that first night he put it with two others to buy bread and fruit and a small flask to fill at the town well, and it was the first money he had ever spent. It took a bronze coin to buy him a small sturdy thonged bag to go under his rags, for his coins. He had taken the bag, and two copper coins as change, from the hand of the craftsman that had made it, but from muffled words between the trader and an older man lounging in the shade beside the stall he knew he had not had full value.

He went out into the scrub and hid well, sleeping warm and dry while his clan searched the town for him. He stayed the next day, and its night, and the day and night after, for he had hidden to overlook the sheltered area where his party always spent their first night on their return journey to the highlands. He had to be sure they had left town before he could return, and, as always, his way of being sure was to see with his own eyes. He watched them for all the time it took them to pitch camp and settle at night and he watched them strike the next morning. Satisfaction it gave him to see which cousin now filled his role, beaten and crying, pegging and fetching and carrying and ranking lower than the pack animals, for it had been his greatest tormentor.

And in those two days of waiting he had for the first time counted his wealth - not counted it as such, for his counting was in the numbering systems used for sheep or wives. He'd had no need yet for the systems for counting money.

Instead, he assessed it in terms of days or months of food, accommodation, clothing, and women (for some of it would be used to experiment there). He knew he had copper coin, and gold coin, and silver coin and bronze. He knew that copper would buy him food, and that the three smallest of those had fed him for two days and would do so for a third. And he knew that copper ranked the least, and then bronze and then silver, and then gold.

He had watched the bidding and the haggling and the paying and the subterfuge of the sheep market and of the tavern and of the brothel through watching and listening to his father and brothers and uncles. And he had almost as much silver and gold as he had copper and bronze. But how much more was the gold worth than the silver or the bronze than the copper? He knew that how he solved that problem would decide his future.

He watched his group leave, mouthed their names as they passed and knew they were all there, that none remained in the town to trap him, by accident or design. He knew they would survive without him, that there were other sons to hammer tent pegs, to be beaten and to take it out on the mindless sheep. He watched the party, all of his blood, grow smaller and smaller in the east, disappear sometimes over a rise and reappear, yet further reduced, nearer the true horizon. With them went his place in society, memory, even his name, for he could call himself anything now, claim any ancestry, any history, and none in the town could from direct knowledge contradict him.

By midday all that he had been had disappeared into the east. He felt no loss, no regrets, as his old identity went with them. He wouldn't need it again. He, or at least his bloodline, had other plans.

Sidoni

We have two churches, chapels, call them what you will. One is high church, sponsored by our imposed state religion, with a wily persuasive priest, less wise than he thinks in the ways of men and of coercion – he humours us, doesn't believe in anything but thinks we do.

Meanwhile we humour him, knowing neither of us gives his god any credence. To him we seem to go there for the festivals of his faith, the ceremonies around the paint-and-plaster saints, and we are good and faithful worshippers enough to satisfy the eye of any itinerant bishop, and we humour him and his church and his parrot-bright saints - to survive.

This religion was not of our choosing.

When its armies came from the south and from the west we wanted none of it – we had our own ways then, older than theirs, older by a thousand years. But we saw what happened to those communities that tried to hold openly to the old ways and to turn aside from the faith the invaders brought to impose on us, proffered on the point of a spear.

Demenos, my old home town, stood up for its faith – and is now only a quarry for worked stone, for timber and tile, for bones and skulls – and an everlasting mine of hatred. Sidoni, too, took a stance before the news came of the death of Demenos and every creature in it, news of the bodies in the streets and in the homes and in our holy places – for the army, in the name of their god, stood guard around the town, now with their newly-cleaned and polished spears and swords, and let in only the bears and the wolves and the foxes and the ravens, until only cracked and polished bone remained. And after this killing our new masters heard of the stance that Sidoni had taken before the news of Demenos could take reason and wisdom there.

From this time, those days, we have new words in our language. The Sidoni Choice is one, to be torn between two equal and compelling choices or forces, as were the men of Sidoni torn between pairs of their own oxen in the name of this unforgiving novice god. And we have the Sidoni Web.

The Web is a weaving pattern, red and black on white, seemingly random, red and black organic shapes, disparate in size, joined by threads of black that meander, perhaps die away to nothing, perhaps appearing to turn a whole circle black. Red is Life, black is Death.

We weave this pattern, for dress fabric, for curtaining, for furnishing, and they, our oppressors, admire it, buy it, and praise it – so delightfully ethnic, they say. We weave it, but they created it.

They wear it, and it shouts their crimes. In the abstract it shows the way they spread death in and from Sidoni. As in Demenos, those deemed to have rejected the imposed belief died, but more slowly, for they were questioned first, of innocent things, marriages, lines of descent, relationships – then the assassins burned out the web-of-life links of which the now newly-dead had been a part.

If a girl had come to Sidoni to marry, say from Kyria on the coast, then those who stalked her and watched her die would know of her parents there, and would go there to interrogate them in turn, and leave them dead, and the sons and daughters of whom they had reminisced, and nephews and nieces and brothers and sisters.

If a son had left to work in the capital of our region he would be followed there, and would die, and in the end his wife and children would welcome death. They burned out the line, leaving the charcoal and ashes shown as black on the Web, in contrast to the red of Life.

They had a logic we could not understand but welcomed – if they found a break in the link caused by the previous death of someone they had pursued they would not kill beyond it, even if they knew names, places, relationships.

You could be betrayed by the presence of living family but not by the dead. And there were some of ours who saw this – and sacrificed themselves, took their own lives to save others, that their deaths would be a barrier against which the killing would stop, beyond which it would not threaten their kin.

These are the black patterns in the Web.

At other times the trail would diminish to a single red thread, the passage of an individual who is free, moving with the winds and the seasons, avoiding the killing of a line and a break in the weave. Such are the single threads that tie the weave together, red representations of those avoiding death by forever travelling, and black for the hunt for, and killing of, the last individual of a line.

I mentioned another chapel, didn't I?

We have our own, hidden from them, somewhere they will never look. Where is it? Safe, safer than you would believe.

In the midnight dark of a day chosen by the calendar of our own, old, faith, we deconsecrated their building, obscenely gaudy as it was and is, and with blood sacrifice and prayer dedicated it to our own gods. Now, of the two chapels, one is the other.

Now, the energy of prayer and genuflection in the name of their interloper god sends energy to ours and takes from theirs. They still search, sometimes, for our worshippers, but they watch and search the caves and grottoes, the cliffs and the high places, where we once bent our knees.

They find nothing. In their great hollow cage of a building, they see us bow and think us tamed, but whatever their priest may be saying we bow only to our old faith and strengthen it by that act.

And one day we will rise and take down them and their emasculated divinity.

Other Musings

A Fictitious Book Review

Azeneth was borne into a tightly defined family in a time of troubles, none of which were permitted to intrude into their insular life. Home, due to the privileges of her father's role within government, was an oasis within a dark, turbulent, world.

Their lives were, to most of their countrymen, a foreign country with manners and mores totally alien to their own. How Cebrian Arroyo Ramirez gained his role as her tutor has been well-explained in his biography by Ovidio Hasdrubal[1], though perhaps this overplays the rumours of a sexual relationship. For a man whose covert political orientation was enough to justify summary execution, it was a remarkable achievement to win a place from which Cebrian could redirect Azeneth's intellectual development. How he utilised this contact with the daughter of a man apparently destined to be, were it not for his early death with the black comedy of its manner, dictator over thirty million people is truly a fascinating subject.

Inevitable changes, accelerated by her father's death and the consequent loss of privilege, destroyed Azeneth's cloistered world.

The Programme of Restitution investigated her family's acquisition of 'their' property. Their sanctuary was confiscated, although no survivors of the dispossessed family came forward to reclaim their original, appropriated, home.

In his later work Hasdrubal[2] recounts Azeneth's reaction to the loss and the discrediting of her kin, and her painful search for justice for survivors of her father's regime, especially the daughter of the missing family, Elí Garcia y Lopez, with whom she shared a birth-year, 1961. Hasdrubal's work was published before this search reached fruition. With the diligence demonstrated throughout her life as a researcher Azeneth located the daughter, still alive in the southern slums, and took responsibility for her housing and education. I will attempt to explain the contradictions in the high-ground stance of Azeneth as the flag-bearer of the liberal left and that of her one-time protégé and friend, Elí, in opposition to her now as the spokeswoman of the extreme right.

1 Cebrian Arroyo – The Hiding Years – Hasdrubal, O. – Oxford University Press – (English tr.) 2001

2 Azeneth – Her Story – Hasdrubal, O. – Oxford University Press – (English tr.) 2004

Birthday Card

A symbol, a reminder of things you would, perhaps, rather forget. Those hurdles, 30, 40, 50 .... But a reminder, also, of things, of people, of feelings you would never want to lose, to forget. And of things you have lost.

'I love you', this one says. 'I love you.' Once her lips could speak the words, repeat the mantra. Now only a card can do it for her. Yellowing now, this one, a reminder of how long it is since she died. Only the writing, in black ink, beautifully cursive, exactly and chillingly like her mother's, can say it. 'I love you - xxx Jay'. And she meant it, oh how she meant it. Born to love, to care, to put others first, to mother. And a wonderful wife she was. She so deserved love in return, and almost always got it.

But when I said 'I love you', if I meant it, it was not to her I spoke. And when she realised that, she died. Not immediately, but like a plant no longer cared for, becoming less, putting out no new shoots, no flower. Just less and less and less, until she wasn't there. And I am nothing without her, for she defined me and now I am less and less and less. And I wish now for there to be the afterlife in which I cannot believe, and a chance to meet her and to tell her the truth – 'I love you'.

Words

I am hiding, Safe, under my rock.

I will not let him use me, abuse me, again.

I am worthy of more than his amateur scratchings.

In the Recording of The Six Days of The Creation I was there, well used, proud of my place.

I am safe here, under my rock, safe from more humiliation at his hand.

Socrates used my foreign sisters and they are respected still!

It is dark here, reassuring. I am safe from his pen.

I trod the stage, helped raise the crowd, for Shakespeare!

I am recorded on vellum, laid there by His goose pen. I have been one with Majesty – how dare he call on me to crawl humbly on his torn pages, as if he owned me, when I have been in the throats of Lear and of Goneril, of Iago and of Desdemona! Even when the Witches used me I was respected!

In the darkness here, no-one can discern me, read me, I am without purpose or function – but better that than being forced to bend my knee to his petty purposes.

I was at Gettysburg! I am one with the founding of America. Lincoln used me, and well, and I am proud that it was so. I am there, on the Address, permanent, with a proper place, proper respect.

And from this stature he has humbled me, reduced me to hiding here, under my stone, least I be called out to perform yet another ludicrous, trivial, role, signifying nothing. How low has he brought me!

I will not be party to his meanderings, his trivia, his ego-enhancement! Rather would I stay here, safe in the dark, and this stone will be my memorial – unless a more worthy master should call me.

I am safe! He has passed me by – some other unfortunate will be his toy today!

Harvesting lives and souls. They have done it since always.

These fresh souls and lives have fed the wind that reaches me, are in it and of it

Is it their fingers that touch my cheek, make the words that dance for me?

What pleases me has taken lives, brought something of those lives towards me – not for my benefit, the wind would be here with its cargo wherever, whenever, whatever I was.

Storm Warning

The air is moving, wonderful, exhilarating in its speed, its force

Pushing at me yet drawing me to its source

It came across the Atlantic, brought with it the air of the Caribbean

It took a yacht under, two humans claimed, never reported, never missed, two lives aborted, two destinies unfulfilled, their spirits travelling now with, and part of, the wind

The power, that lion-roar, of the storm pulled me from my bed, a crime to have stayed there, ignoring its presence, its majesty

A hundred miles west of me its power has felled a yew

Taken from it a quarter of a millennium of life,

One-eighth of A.D.

I am walking without purpose, without specific goal, solely to feel the wind's touch on my cheek, the tears it draws from my eyes

That yew crushed a car, killing a mother and her child,

Much shorter lives

The wind pleasures my soul, writing rhymes and rhythms in
my head

Making words join and dance for me alone

It is my friend, my inspiration, my ally.

Further west a boy, young, still at that 'immortal' age

Faces, challenges, the storm, along an unprotected pier

Daring his older, wiser, friends to follow him

He dies – the wind and sea work well together

Notice Of A Dastardly Crime

(*Poemtry* Has This Day Been Committed)

News has reached this office that words, INNOCENT words, have been taken from their homes, indeed from their very beds, ripped from their families, BASTARDISED!!.

It seems their assent was assumed, taken for granted, their will overridden.

In this CRIMIINAL ACT they have been emasculated. Without their leave they have been abbreviated, truncated, amputated. Adverbs and nouns have been reshaped as adjectives and interjections.

Forced unwilling into a mould, their shape taken from them, their birth-right denied, their very continued existence in doubt. In the misuse and abuse they have suffered they have had their true power ignored, taken from them.

They have been trivialised, made to serve a lesser purpose. Words made great by Shakespeare have been made as nothing in the hands of CRIMINAL!

They cry out for our support, our aid, in their rescue. They are asking only to be returned to their rightful homes. But, for them, for those whose voice is small and unheard and

Oh!

without power, we must ask for more, for the punishment of the perpetrator of these crimes, nay, THESE SINS!

He is known to you, and to us all, for his trivial, puerile, scratchings and pontifications, and against him we demand JUSTICE, we demand

ACTION - NOW!

Acknowledgments

I would personally like to thank the following people who assisted in the creation of this book:

Tracy, Sian, Becky, Meg, Codie and Mary.

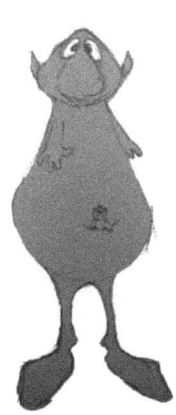

... and that was Oh!

Publisher: Independent Publishing Network.

Publication date: 31 August 2021

ISBN: ISBN: 978-1-80068-140-8

Author: George Austin Wills

Email: georgewills99@yahoo.com

Please direct all enquiries to the author.

Lightning Source UK Ltd.

Lightning Source UK Ltd.
Milton Keynes UK
UKHW020411140921
390506UK00001B/20

9 781800 681408